That Extra Scratch

Behind the Ear

Nails

Chapter #1 - Nail Inspection

A lot of Vets, Groomers and Owners don't like or are afraid to trim dog nails, especially the black ones because they cut them too short, hit the quick and the dog is bleeding and in pain. The fussing, whining, yipping, struggling and biting begins because…damn it, that hurts when the quick is cut! Plus dogs do remember exactly which nail was cut too short because they are cool and calm with the other nails being trimmed and suddenly start to fuss and pull back over one nail.

So from this paragraph on read carefully more than once because this is how to trim nails without pain or blood all the time!

First of all, pull the hair back off the nail area and really look at the nails.

Inspection:

1. The colour of the nails.

2. The length of the nails.

3. Where is the quick?

4. Is the quick even or uneven throughout **all** the nails? (Yes, even the black ones, keep reading and the mystery of the black nails will be revealed!!)

5. Check the angle of wear on the nail tips this indicates the way the dog walks off its pads and onto the nail.

6. Check to see if the toe and nail twist to the side or is the toe arched up due to nail length.

7. Check for broken nails.

8. If there is a broken nail, check for inflammation or tenderness around the nail bed and toe.

9. Check for dew claws on all four feet, this check is very important because ... Some dew claws and some nails will curve and grow into the toe pad causing a lot of pain and infections. Finally,

10. Watch the dog's response to this quick but thorough inspection. Do they pull back their paws? Do they table dance and start to twist? Do they snap? If snapping, be prepared to muzzle the dog while you work on the nails and feet trimming, for both your protection. Put a drop of lavender oil on the top of the muzzle to help calm the dog.

This inspection takes very little time and is very important because the feet are the dog's foundation and poor nail care can radiate pain up the legs to the rest of the dog's body. Ask anyone with sore feet where they hurt because they are compensating for those sore tootsies?

The dog will let you know the nails are too long by the ticking on the floor, by the rusty orange lick spots on the toes and lower legs and feet or some dogs will chew their nails because they are too long.

Chapter #2 - Nail Colour and the Quick

There are five colours of nails, black, white, burgundy, striped black and white and striped burgundy and white. These stripes are vertical and follow the nail shape from nail bed to tip.

Black Nails

We'll start with the worst colour first, Black. Owners, Vets and Groomers alike hate cutting the black nails because they can't see the quick. Ahh, but take another look, the quick **is** visible, really.

Take a good look at the black nail. For the moment, ignore the quick inside the nail. Look at the outside of the black nail closely. The nail coming from the nail bed is nice and smooth, shiny even. Then the nail starts to look scored and dull ½ to ¾ of the way down the nail towards the tip. This is your **demarcation line**. This line is **jagged and uneven** but it does circle around the black nail. **Some are very faint** but it will still be there around the nail.

Cut the nail **below** the **lowest point** on the demarcation line. That is the safe zone on a black nail, because the quick is in the shiny half. Turn the toe so you can see the bottom of the cut nail, can you see a **small** round circle in the center of the nail? If so do not cut any more as that is the beginning of the quick, the smaller the center circle the safer the quick is. The bigger the center circle in the nail, the closer and more painful you are to bleeding the quick. **Be very careful.** If there is no **small** center circle in the nail tip and it is all white, trim the nail in thin increments till you can see the **small** center circle.

Hold it!! Now before you start blissfully trimming all the black nails in site you will find that the odd dog will have this in the reverse. That odd dog will have the dullness coming from the nail bed and the smooth shiny black on the tips. This reverse is caused by poor diet or health and shows in the nails and hair first. The same cut still applies. Cut **below** the **lowest point** on the demarcation line.

Hold on hold on, there is one more type of black nail that is really different. It's the totally black shiny nail with a white tip at the end. Cut **only** the white tip because the **quick is really long**. The white tip is the old nail that the colour has leached out, because it grew past the nourishing quick.

Ok, now you can safely cut all the black nails you could ever want!

White, Black and White, Burgundy, Burgundy and White Nails

On all of these nail colours the rule of thumb is to look at the sides of the nail before you cut, to see where the tip of the quick rests because the quick will be deceiving on some dogs nails. The quick will extend further out along the bottom of the nail then at the top. That's the reason you end up making the easy white nails bleed because you are going by the top of the nail not the bottom. So you will have to cut further down the tip by using an angle \, (back slash) way past the start of the solid white in order to miss the angled quick. This angle \ cut encourages the quick to recede on the bottom by removing the protective top part of the nail. It will take two or three trims on this angle to correct the growth of the quick so that you are then able to make a, l (vertical cut) and keep the nails short.

Some white nails are only white at the very tip of the nail because the quick is so far down the nail that the entire nail looks pink. Only trim the white tip but cut it on a / (forward slash) angle.

These different angles are used to correct and make uniform the quick in every nail. The quick will recede back up the nail and allow more nail tip to be cut off next trimming. Some dogs only need to have this angling done one or two times, some dogs need it done more to encourage the quick to recede.

Ok, I have to add another type of nail to this list because I had a new client come to my salon three times now and low and behold this dog's nails were banded **horizontally!!** All the striped nails I've done were vertical. This dog's nail bands were black and cream and black and burgundy and only ¼ inch wide bands of colours. So I checked the sides of the nails and yes you could see the quick and I found that I only had to cut one band of colour on each of the nails.

Is this a new self-preservation evolution for dogs? The body pre-marks the nails so silly humans only cut one band at a time to prevent pain and bleeding? We can only dream.

How often should the nails be trimmed?

Ok folks, this is the answer that every Dog Owner needs to know: You need to trim your dog's nails **every three to four weeks** depending on your dog's metabolism (fast or slow growth). In the spring time your dog's nails will suddenly, overnight become eagle talons. This is because your dog is reducing the energy needed to stay warm, especially in colder climates and increasing the energy in the regenerative areas, nails and summer coat regrowth. Some of my clients come in every two weeks in the spring because the nails grow so fast. So literally play it by ear, when you hear the ticking on the floor it's time for a nail trim. Or lift the dog's paw up like a horses hoof. Do the nails extend past the toe pad? Yes? Then they need to be trimmed. The nails, looking at the paw in profile, should sit half way down the toe pad. This stops the ticking on the floor, foot pain etc. and still allows dig in when the dog runs.

Chapter #3 - The 'Routine' and Handling the Paw

The nails are the worst part of grooming for the Trimmer and the dog. So, you get the worst over with first, then, the rest of the grooming session will be relatively stress free and easy in comparison.

Adjust the table height. Have the client face you on the table. Hold the **Right front paw** in your hand between your pointer and tall man. Using your thumb, push the hair up and away from the nail. Start with the **dew claw** and then the inside nail working your way to the outside nail. Then do the same with the **Left Front paw,** then the **Left Back paw** and the **Right Back paw.** Always, check each paw for **dew claws.** Some dew claws sit higher than others and some hide in the hair. The dew claws on some crossbred or poorly bred dogs have been found **almost beside** the other nails or **behind** the foot, not on the inside of the lower ankle.

Praise the dog for co-operating with each nail that is trimmed. Always position the client so you have maximum access to each paw.

1. Keep to the 'Routine' R.F. L.F. L.B. R.B. as this will help you with accuracy and then speed. Learn to be accurate first. Then pick up your speed. Speed before accuracy causes injuries, not only to the dog but to you as well.

2. Sticking to the 'Routine' enables the client to become familiar with it as well. Some clients will anticipate the next move by turning into the next position and lifting

the next paw. This is fabulous because TRUST has been established as well as the 'Routine' and the beginnings of good communication and co-operation. The client remembers the 'Routine' and is comfortable with it and you. Don't forget to praise the dog when he anticipates.

Small to Medium Dogs

The best way to trim small to medium dog nails is on the grooming table. Have the owner remove the leash. Lift the dog properly onto the table. Raise or lower the table to a comfortable height. Double lanyard the dog for safety. Start with the 'Routine', be sure to check and trim the dew claws. **Do not cut any nails if the dog is pulling back its leg or dancing around the table.** Triple strap the dog (two lanyards and a collar through the back lanyard to the grooming arm), in this case to safely prevent excess movement of the dog then proceed with the trimming. Another way is to turn the dog away from you and snug his back side against your chest, lift the paws like a horses hooves. Or have the owner snug the dog's head in the crook of their elbow and the dog's body snug across their chest while you trim their nails, pads up. Another way is to hook a finger into the dog's collar and hold the paw in the same hand. This allows absolutely no pull back and the dog seems to calm down quickly.

Some dogs are more comfortable with these ways of trimming because they can't see. When trimming the stressed dog, calmly, using low voice inflection, praise the dog after each nail has been trimmed. **Do not let the paw go**. Hold on to the paw and gently rub the toe you just trimmed, between your thumb and finger of your free hand. Move on to the next toe nail trim and praise. This retraining method shows the dog that every time they hold still they get praised when the nail is trimmed. The dog will build up its confidence and trust in you as their pawdicurist and eventually just sit or stand while their nails are trimmed. Yes, they will because I have a whack load of nail clients that fussed, fought, bit etc. because they'd been hurt by others during previous nail trims and now they just stand or sit while I trim their nails.

** Recently I have been asking the owners to snug the dogs/cats back into their chest and have all four paws facing me. I quickly snip the nails and the fuss have been extremely minimal this has worked on fussy large dogs as well with the owner sitting in a chair and the large dogs hind feet on the floor. The large dogs back snugged into the owners chest, the owner holds the dogs head up with one hand and slowly scrubs the dog's chest with the other. This position is like swaddling clothes for the dog and they remain calmer, you can see the nails a lot better, better visibility allows the nails to get trimmed so much faster because there is less struggling by the dog, plus all four feet are right there in the open.

Trimming Larger Dog Nails

Strap on your knee pads and have the owner sit in a comfy chair. Have the dog sit in front of the owner. Take the leash off. The owner holds the collar, keeping the muzzle up and scrubs the chest area slowly and calmly. Using the same 'Routine', right front, left front etc. leave the feet on the floor and trim the tips below the quick. Open the trimmers wide to go around the nail on the floor. This method allows proper trimming and ensures space between the nails and the floor. Or you can place the paw on your knee, especially the back paws as this will help the dog keep their balance.

No ticking, no pain and no bleeding. Also there is less stress and fighting with a large strong dog that pulls back its paw.

Also large dogs can lie down or sit as you lift each paw to be trimmed. Read the dog and apply the method that suits.

Nail trimming should take no more than 3-5 minutes tops, fighting and dancing included. Because it only takes a short time, nail trimming should be a walk-in service, no appointment necessary.

Groomers and Vets nail trimming is a **necessity for dogs.**
Don't over price something that is so important to a dog's
health and physical mobility. Between eight to ten dollars
should only be charged on this vital service. I know, who is she
to tell me how much to charge for my work? But, you know
what to look for in all the nail colours and how to trim them
properly. One nail trim, eight to ten dollars, every three weeks,
for 3-5 minutes each visit, over a year will net you a nice profit.
Now picture a nice solid 50+ dogs just for nails. Everybody wins
in the end. The dog gets a nice pain and blood free nail
trimming on a regular basis, the owner's wallet isn't gouged,
which will encourage the owner to bring the dog back more
often, plus they'll spread the word. It's quick, clean, no pain, no
blood and the dog is in and out again and you get a regular nail
client.

Chapter #4 - Extra Stuff You Need to Know

Sedation to Trim Nails?!!

What?! If you have to sedate the **average to the 'fear of pain, aggressive'** dog to have its nails trimmed, the person trimming the nails is doing it **wrong.** Sedation of any kind is hard on the dog's system, stressful to the owner, not to mention expensive $35.00 to $65.00 to have this type of nail trimming done. What's wrong with this picture? Have that person read this book on the proper way to trim nails because I have dealt with aggressive dogs re: their nails and with this 'Routine' and verbal reprimands and or muzzles, plus remaining calm, lots of lavender oil and the owner watching the whole process, these dogs can and very definitely have learned to trust me to trim their nails properly. **Please note that I have refused to trim only a few dogs nails/grooming because the owner could not/would not control their 'pet' and it got out of the required muzzle needed to minimize any damage it would cause. These few refusals were small as well as large dogs and these refusals do not reflect poorly on my ability, but does reflect on the owner's lack of responsibility in properly training their 'pet'.

Nail Trimmers, Which Style is better?

The best pair of trimmers is a sharp pair. I prefer the scissor style. It allows me to see the entire nail and quick as I am cutting. I use the medium size for all size dogs because they fit comfortably in my hand and allow me to trim quickly. Remove the wire latch that holds the trimmers closed when not in use because it can flip and lock the trimmers while you are trying to cut and it will also pinch your palm as you trim. That hurts.

Some groomers, vets or owners prefer the dremil tool to file down the dog's nails. They are good **but** you have to **be careful** because they heat up the nail quickly causing the nail to burn. The same as a dremil tool at a lady's nail salon**, they burn**. So be careful and check the heat level on the nail often by touching the nail with your thumb. Only touch the dremil file to the nail in short quick touches to prevent excess heat build-up. Get a dremil tool that has a variable speed and go slow till you become proficient with this tool.

One last tool in your nail trimming arsenal is an 80/100 grit nail file. You can cut the files in half for the larger dogs or in thirds for small to medium size dogs. All you have to do is file the nail edge once or twice to dull the sharpness. This is a boon in the summer time for the owners who have bare legs and feet.

For those of you who own cats, birds, rodents and reptiles with legs, use the 10 step Quick Inspection and trimming Routine on these pets as well. Using a long handled cat nail trimmer is the perfect size trimmers for their nails.

Thank you for putting your pet's feet first.

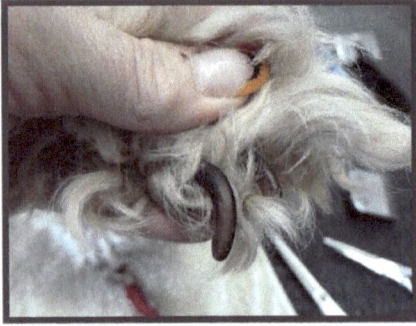

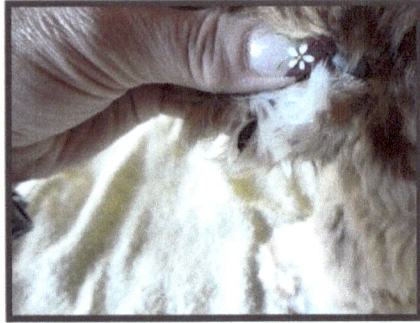

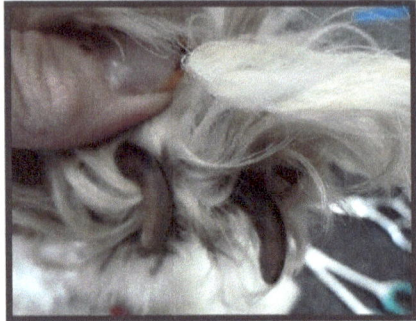

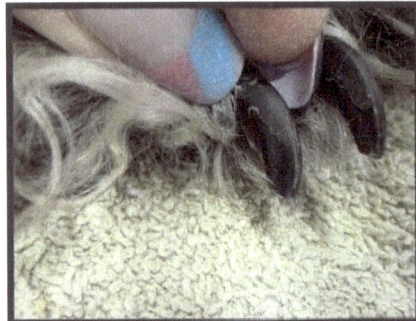

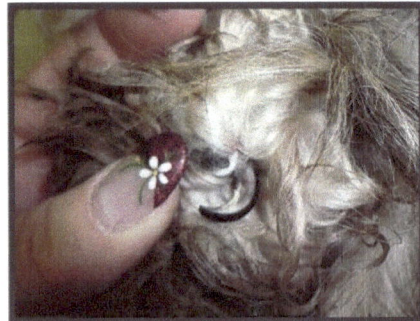

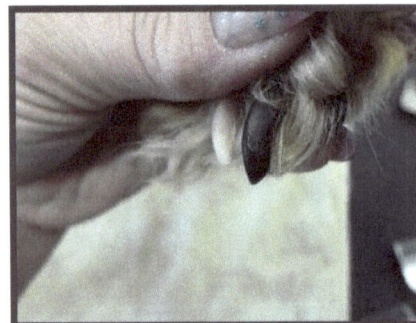

That Extra Scratch Behind the Ear - Nails

Nails

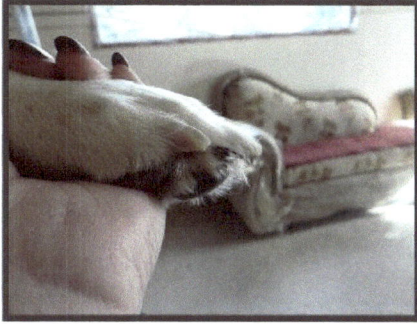

Properly trimmed nails sit above toe pads

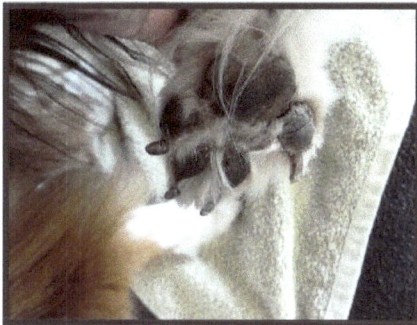

Nails so long the toes
become splayed and twisted

Planters wart and worn twisted nails

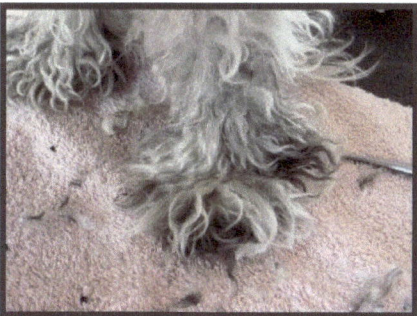

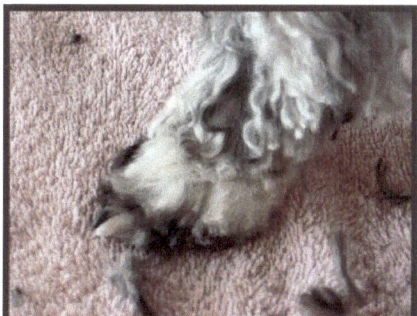

That Extra Scratch Behind the Ear - Nails

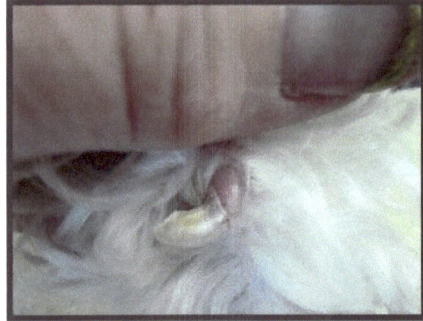

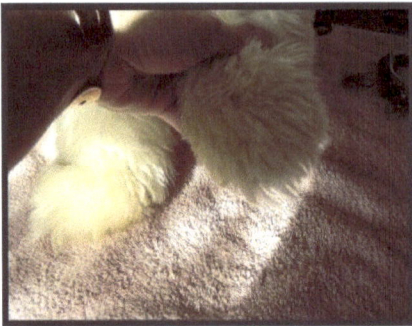

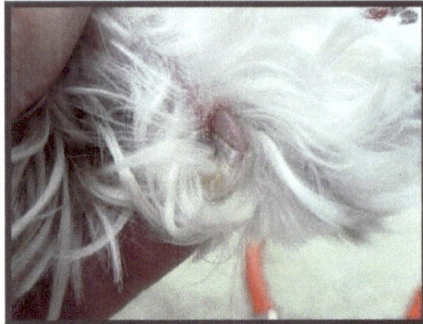

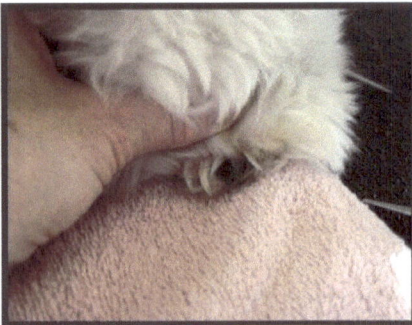

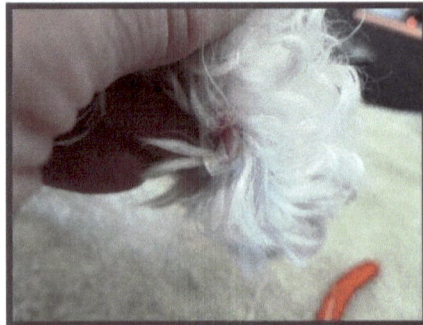

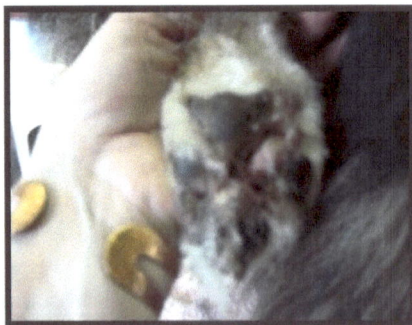

Broken nail past the quick
and broken nail trimmed

That Extra Scratch Behind the Ear - Nails

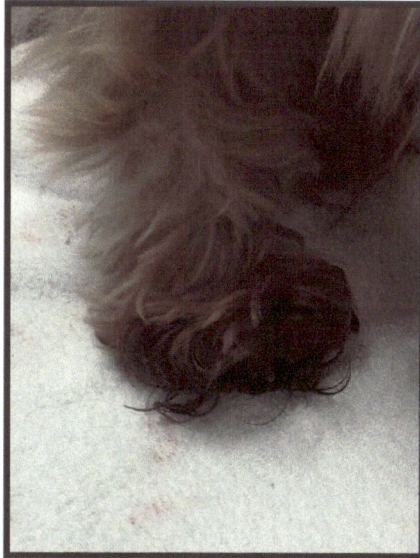

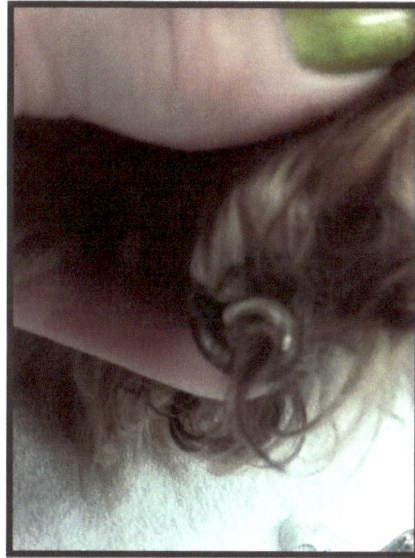

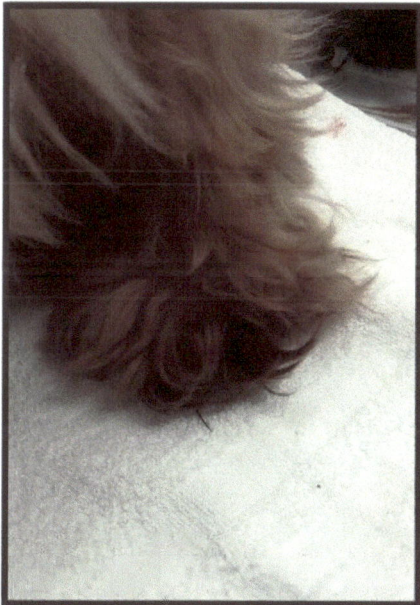

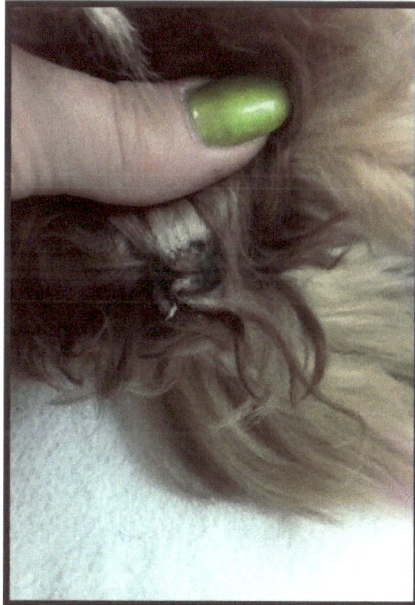

That Extra Scratch Behind the Ear - Nails

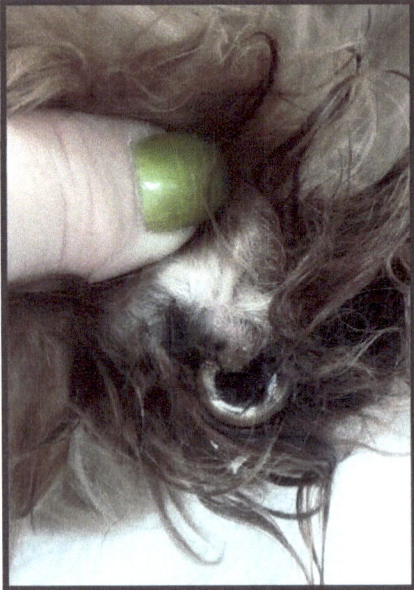

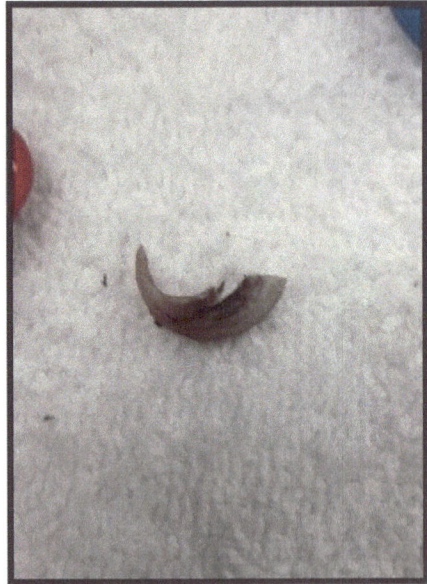

Barbed nail removed

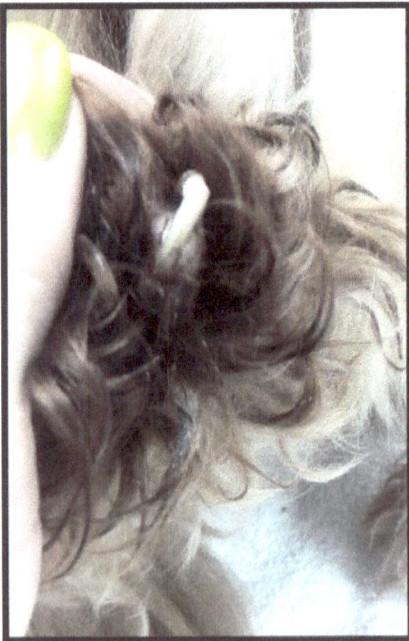

Imbedded barbed nail in toe pad

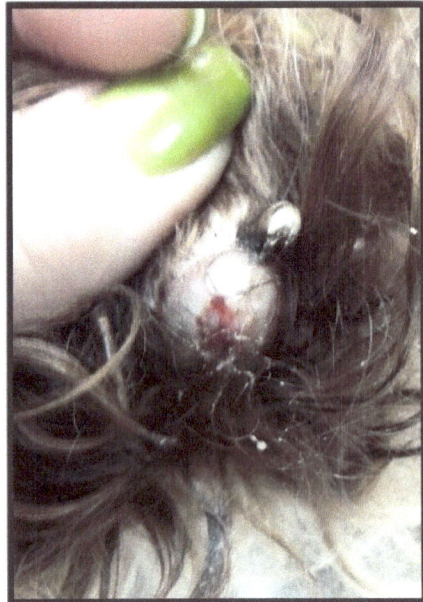

That Extra Scratch Behind the Ear - Nails

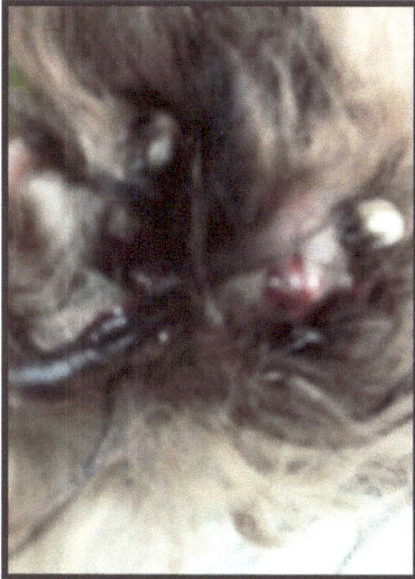

Nails trimmed and pulled out of toe pads
which were bleeding and infected

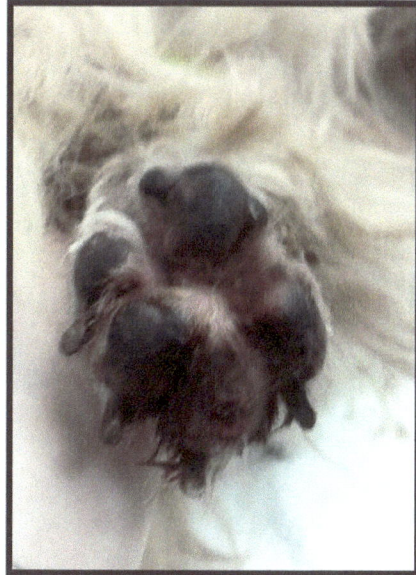

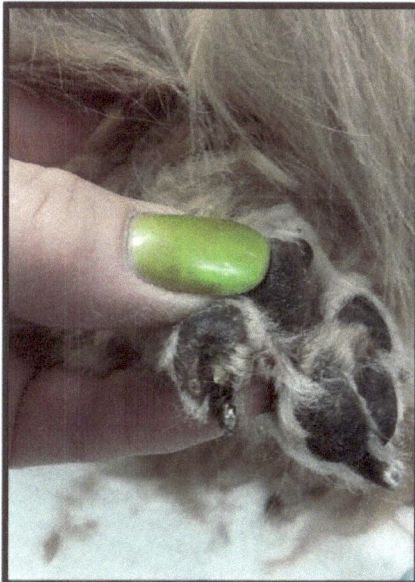

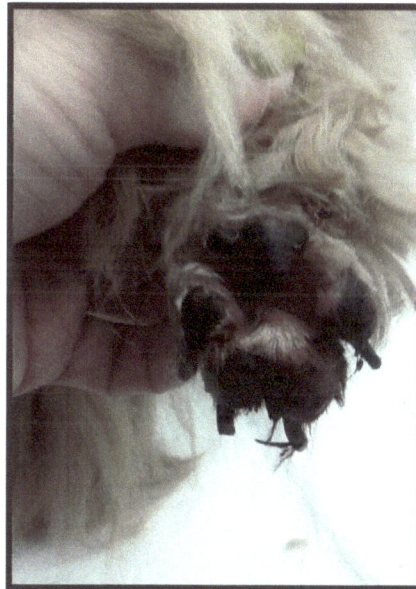

Nails imbedded in toe pads and in the skin
between pads and yes this was
reported to the S.P.C.A

That Extra Scratch Behind the Ear - Nails

www.ingramcontent.com/pod-product-compliance
Lightning Source LLC
Chambersburg PA
CBHW061059090426
42742CB00002B/90